JEFF FOXWORTHY'S

REDNECK
DICTIONARY

II

JEFF FOXWORTHY'S

REDNECK DICTIONARY

II

More Words You Thought
You Knew the Meaning Of

JEFF FOXWORTHY

with FAX BAHR, ADAM SMALL,
GARY CAMPBELL, AND BRIAN HARTT

Illustrations by LAYRON DEJARNETTE

VILLARD NEW YORK

Published in the United States by Villard Books, an imprint of The Random House Publishing Group, a division of Random House, Inc., New York.

VILLARD and "V" CIRCLED Design are registered trademarks of Random House, Inc.

ISBN 1-4000-6568-2

Printed in the United States of America on acid-free paper

www.villard.com

987654321

First Edition

Book design by Susan Turner

JEFF FOXWORTHY'S

REDNECK
DICTIONARY

ADEQUATE

Aa

ac·cus·tom (ə-kəs´-təm), *n. and v.* to have verbally abused more than one person with profanity. *"Them kids kept swearin' around Mamaw, so **accustom** out."*

ad·e·quate (a´-də-kwit), *n. and v.* to have acted with the intention of terminating one's condition of employment. *"**Adequate** if they hadn't given me a raise."*

Af·ghan·i·stan (af-gan´-is-stan), *n. and v.* to declare that a certain living organism of Afghani origin has the name Stanley. *"The Dalmatian's called Jerry, but the **Afghanistan**."*

agent (ā´-jənt), *n. and v.* to negate the importance of the length of a thing's existence. *"She may be eighty, but if I'm drunk enough, **agent** make no difference to me."*

Aleve (ə-lēvʹ), *n. and v.* to intend to vacate. *"Sure Aleve, bud . . . soon as I finish off this six-pack."*

al·lo·sau·rus (aʹ-lə-sȯrʹ-əs), *n. and v.* to have been visually perceived by someone named Alice. *"I think my wife allosaurus go into that motel room together."*

al·lure (ə-lürʹ), *n.* an object used for enticement, with the intention of capturing prey. *"You want to catch a fish, you gotta use allure."*

an·a·con·da (an-ə-känʹ-də), *n. and v.* to have swindled by gaining the confidence of the victim. *"I robbed a bank, stole a car, anaconda old lady out of her life savings."*

ALLURE

AORTA

an·nu·al (an´-yü-əl), *n. and v.* regarding the prediction of an action. *"Buy this here Porsche **annual** be dating a lot of ladies."*

an·te·lope (ant´-ə-lōp), *n. and v.* the female sibling of one's parent escaping, with the intention of betrothal. *"Sure it's cool to help yer **antelope**, but it ain't cool if she's gettin' hitched to you."*

aor·ta (ā-ȯr´-tə), *n. and v.* involving a suggestion for action. *"**Aorta** tear that house down and start over."*

apart·ment (ə-pärt´-mənt), *adv. and v.* pertaining to one's feelings about a separation. *"Our time together was real good, but the time we were **apartment** a lot more to me."*

ap·par·el (ə-per´-əl), *n. and v.* a prediction concerning the future of two things. *"When it comes to shoes, **apparel** look better than just the one."*

ap·peal (ə-pēl´), *n.* medicine in a form for oral ingestion. *"I'm sorry, sir, this is not **appeal** you swallow. It's the kind you take rectally."*

ar·rest (ə-rest´), *n.* a state of minimal activity. *"I want the cops to lock me up 'cause, frankly, I could use **arrest**."*

as·cent (ə-sent´), *n. and v.* to have personally dispatched. *"Please don't turn off my phone, dude . . . I swear **ascent** that check three weeks ago!"*

APPEAL

ASUNDER

as·sas·sin (ə-saˊ-sən), *v.* disrespecting verbally. *"Don't just stand there **assassin** me, boy—go clean your room!"*

asun·der (əs-ənˊ-dər), *n. and prep.* a gluteal mass situated below or beneath. *"You'll need a tarp-sized blanket to get all of her **asunder** it."*

at·tract (ə-traktˊ), *v.* to have followed. *"I must **attract** that deer for six miles before I gave up."*

aw·ful (ȯ-fəlˊ), *adv. and adj.* satiated gastronomically. *"No dessert for me, thanks, I'm **awful**."*

Bb

ban·dit (band´-ət), *v. and n.* censured or forbidden, by decree. *"We can't dance no more, 'cause after the preacher saw* Footloose, *he **bandit**."*

bar·gain (bär´-gən), *n. and adv.* pertaining to a return to a tavern. *"I'm still thirsty, so whaddya say we go hit that **bargain**."*

bas·tards (bas´-tərds), *n.* the fecal excretions of any animal of the Centrarchidae, Serranidae, or Percichthyidae families. *"I'll bet you'll catch a bunch where all them black specks is floatin', 'cause them black specks is **bastards**."*

bet·ter·ment (be´-tər-mənt), *v. aux. and v.* demanding a certain or particular intention. *"I'm not sure I heard you right. You **betterment** that you were gonna marry my little girl."*

BETTERMENT

BIGAMY

big·a·my (big´-ə-mē), *adj. and n.* a boastful procla-
mation of one's actions as generous. *"It was pretty*
bigamy *to pick up the dinner check for all of my ex-wives."*

bi·son (bī´-sən), *interj. and n.* used to express
farewell to a male offspring. *"The day I went off to*
welding school, Mama stood on the porch with tears in
*her eyes and said, '****Bison****.' "*

boil (bȯi´-əl), *interj. and v.* a term preceding a prediction. *"****Boil*** *they be surprised when they find out I ain't*
dead."

bot·a·ny (bät´-ən-ē), *v. and conj.* used to describe
the reaction of a male person to a purchase, usually by
his spouse. *"When she got back from the mall, she*
showed him what she ***botany*** *killed himself."*

butch·er (bŭ´-chər), *v. and adj.* to place or lay an object or objects belonging to another. *"If you don't want a fist in your face, you better **butcher** cards on the table."*

but·ter (bət´-ər), *conj. and adj.* with the exception of an action by or quality of a female. *"She may be nice on the eyes, **butter** cookin'll kill ya."*

but·ton fly (bət´-in-flī), *n. and v.* to elevate one's posterior above the ground. *"The mother bird just told her baby to get off its **button fly**."*

Cc

Cae·sar (sēz´-ər), *v. and n.* to visually perceive a female. *"He has a seizure every time he **Caesar**."*

BUTTER

CANADA

Can·a·da (kan´-ə-də), *n. and prep.* a metal container with specific contents. *"Do me a big favor, bud,
and hand me a **Canada** bug spray."*

can·cel (kant´-səl), *v.* the inability to exchange
property for money. *"If you **cancel** that hunk of crap, I'll
take it off your hands."*

can·cer (kan´-sər), *v. and n.* to formally acknowl-
edge one's abilities. *"He asked if I could be there by eight
o'clock and I said, 'Yes, I **cancer**.' "*

can·nel·lo·ni (kan-əl-ō´-nē), *n. and v.* the limit to
a metal container's capacity. *"That **cannelloni** hold
about two cups of water."*

cash·ew (ka´-shü), *v. and n.* to exchange chips for hard currency. *"I wanted to keep gambling, but the manager said, 'I think we'd better **cashew** in.' "*

CAT scan (kats´-kan), *n. and v.* pertaining to the abilities of members of the feline family. *"No way my dogs are getting on this here couch, but my **CAT scan**."*

cau·ter·ize (kȯt´-ər-īz), *v. and n.* to visually engage a female person's ocular organs. *"It was love at first sight the second I **cauterize**."*

cel·lu·lite (sel´-yü-līt), *v. and adj.* to make a mercantile exchange wherein a food or beverage product of reduced caloric content is traded for currency. *"We're outta regular Bud, but I could **cellulite** beer."*

CAT SCAN

CHARITY

char·i·ty (char´-ə-tē), *n. and pron.* a restrictive clause relating to a male person's actions concerning a piece of furniture providing an individual seat. *"That fat boy breaks every **charity** sits in."*

chick·en (chik´-in), *n. and conj.* a connection between a female person and something else. *"I went to the movies with that **chicken** Maynard . . . next thing I know, we was makin' out."*

colt (kōlt´), *adj.* having an unpleasantly low temperature. *"I'll say it's **colt** out here, man. . . . When I got back to the barn, my dang horse was frozen solid!"*

com·fort (kəm´-fərt), *v. and adv.* to move toward, with the aim of procurement. *"That fellah that left his dog here . . . I hope he'll **comfort** soon."*

con·ceal (kən-sēl´), *v.* to be able to cover tightly. *"If you **conceal** up that window, a lot less bugs'll get in."*

con·ceit (kən-sēt´), *v.* to be able to accommodate resting places for buttocks. *"Our high school football stadium **conceit** fifty thousand."*

con·trol (kən-trōl´), *v.* to be able, while moving slowly, to display a lure for the purpose of capture. *"You **control** in this lake for a week, and you still ain't gonna catch a fish."*

copy (käp´-ē), *n. and pron.* regarding an action by a male person concerning a law enforcement officer. *"I hope we don't run into the **copy** shot at."*

CONTROL

COUNTY

coun·ty (kaŭnt´-ē), *v. and n.* to combine integers, as done by a male person. *"To **county** has to take off his shoes, if you want him to get past ten."*

cra·ter (krā´-tər), *n.* the Supreme Being, responsible for bringing forth all things known and unknown. *"Come Judgment Day, all you sinners are gonna have to answer to the **crater**!"*

Dd

Da·ko·ta (də-kō´-tə), *n. and v.* a prediction concerning an outer garment worn on the torso. *"It's ten below, man. **Dakota** keep you warm."*

da·ta (dāt´-ə), *v. and adj.* to undertake an event of social interaction, usually with the purpose of romance. *"I'd never **data** rich girl."*

de·men·tia (dim-ent´-shə), *n. and v.* interrogative concerning one's reaction to, or connection with, more than one person. *"You lookin' at **dementia**?"*

dem·on·strate (dem´-ən-strāt), *n. and adj.* in a linear fashion. *"Your glasses are all crooked, girl . . . put **demonstrate**."*

dis·abil·i·ty (dis-ə-bi´-lə-tē), *adj. and n.* a certain aptitude or proficiency. *"I was born with **disability** to charm women of the opposite sex."*

dis·cov·er (dis-kə´-vər), *adj. and n.* a particular object on or over something or used to protect it. *"I couldn't find baby Boo for the life of me, till I lifted **discover**."*

DEMENTIA

DISROBE

dis·ease (diz-ēz´), *v. and adj.* interrogative concerning more than one thing. *"I been sick for nine years, Doc. **Disease** pills work or not?"*

dis·fig·ured (dis-fi´-gyərd), *adv. and v.* to have ascertained. *"I **disfigured** you would go with me instead of him."*

dis·robe (dis-rōb´), *adj. and n.* a particular full-length long-sleeved garment, usually worn over pajamas. *"How come you always make me take **disrobe** off in the dark, sweetie?"*

dis·taste (dis-tāst´), *n. and v.* regarding the distinctive flavor of a specific thing. *"Is it just me, or does **distaste** funny?"*

dis·trict (dis´-trikt), *adv. and adj.* severe in terns of discipline. *"I never woulda joined up if I'd known the army was gonna be **district**."*

dit·ty (dit´-ē), *v. and n.* interrogative concerning the past actions of a male person. *"Let me guess: your husband never learned how do swim, **ditty**?"*

doc·u·ment (däk´-yə-mənt), *n. and v.* an intended medical professional. *"First you said Dr. Reynolds did it, and now you're saying that ain't the **document**."*

dog·ma (dȯg´-mə), *v. and adj.* to personally insult something belonging to one. *"I had to hit him, sir—I ain't just gonna sit there and let a man **dogma** truck."*

DITTY

DWARF

doz·en (dəz´-ən), *v. and adv.* the negative or opposite of an expected action or reaction. *"If that **dozen** make you laugh, then you don't know what's funny."*

drain (drān´), *n.* precipitation. *"**Drain** in Spain falls mainly on the plain."*

dwarf (dwȯrf´), *n.* a structure built alongside or on a body of water for the purpose of parking watercraft. *"We can fish down at **dwarf**."*

dy·na·mite (dī´-nə-mīt), *v. and n.* concerning expiration and one's subsequent action or reaction. *"I know blowing up this safe is dangerous. I might **dynamite** not."*

easy·go·ing (ē-zē-gō´-ing), *v. and n.* interrogative regarding the future movements or trajectory of a male. *"**Easygoing** to relax or not?"*

Egypt (ē´-jipt), *n. and v.* to have been cheated or swindled by a male. *"Aw, man, **Egypt** me!"*

em·bit·ter (im-bi´-tər), *n. and adj.* when a male feels resentful, angry, vengeful, and soured. *"His divorce just left **embitter**."*

en·dive (en-dīv´), *conj. and v.* to leap or plunge, especially in a headlong manner. *"Just walk to the edge of the board **endive** off."*

ENDIVE

ERODE

erec·tor (i-rekt´-ər), *n. and v.* to have destroyed or rendered useless; as done by a male. *"Tom's wife is mad at him 'cause **erector** new car."*

er·go (ər´-gō), *n. and v.* a female moving off on a specific course. *"I want to take my girlfriend camping, but I don't think her dad's gonna let **ergo**."*

erode (i-rōd´), *n. and v.* a male person on a thing that moved him around physically. *"Old man Wilkins is losing it, dude. **Erode** that dang pig all the way to town."*

es·crow (es´-krō), *v.* to suggest the instigation of the natural process wherein a seedling advances in size. *"**Escrow** some tomatoes this summer."*

eu·pho·ria (yü-fȯr´-ē-ə), *n.* form of address for a group consisting of a number of persons between three and five. *"Hey!* **Euphoria** *ain't going nowhere till you clean up that mess!"*

ex·tinct (ek-stinkt´), *n. and v.* the olfactory unpleasantness of one's former spouse. *"My new wife smells okay, but my* **extinct** *real bad."*

eye·sore (ī-sȯr´), *n. and v.* a first-person declaration of a visual perception. *"Back off, man,* **eyesore** *first!"*

Ff

fairy (fer´-ē), *adj. and n.* a description for a male person of light complexion and pigmentation. *"Jim's so* **fairy** *gets sunburned as soon as he goes outside."*

EXTINCT

FIRED

feed (fēd´), *conj. and n.* the conditional desire for a male to act. *"I'd kick his butt, **feed** just step outside."*

fil·i·greed (fil-ə-grēd´), *n. and v.* consent and acceptance by a person named Phillip. *"I said we should kick him out of the club, and **filigreed**."*

fired (fī´-ərd), *conj. and v.* interrogative about the correct aural perception of a meaning. *"**Fired** you right, you want me to give you my wallet?"*

fis·sure (fish´-ər), *n. and v.* regarding the actions of an aquatic creature. *"Ever since the earthquake, the **fissure** really bitin'."*

fist (fist´), *conj. and v.* the possible meaning of a state of being or of an action. *"**Fist** a first offense I'll let you go, but **fist** the second one, and **fist** for fightin', your butts are going to jail."*

fluo·ride (flòr´-īd), *n. and v.* a hypothetical personal action concerning the lowest horizontal plane of a room. *"If that was my **fluoride** mop it."*

fly·er (flī´-ər), *n.* a blossoming reproductive shoot of a sporophytic organism. *"Let's swing by the cemetery so I can lay a **flyer** on Grandma's grave."*

for·ti·fy (fort´-əf-ī), *n. and conj.* concerning possible action toward an enclosed structure used for protection. *"I wouldn't attack that **fortify** was you."*

FORTIFY

FORTUNES

for·tu·itous (fȯr-tü´-ət-əs), *prep. and n.* a declaration that a thing is intended for only a pair. *"Luckily, that sofa ain't so good for three people, but **fortuitous**."*

for·tunes (fȯr´-chəns), *adj. and n.* the quadripartite region formed by the lower jaw of a particularly fleshy face. *"When Bill was just fat, he had two chins. But now that he's obese, he's got **fortunes**."*

free·dom (frē´-dəm), *adj. and n.* a triumvirate. *"Y'all better take a cookie now, 'cause dey's only **freedom** left."*

freeze (frēz´), *n. and v.* a declaration concerning the state of a male individual. *"**Freeze** a jolly good fellow!"*

Gg

gal·lon (gal´-ən), *n. and prep.* a reference to the location of a female person. *"The one with the jug is ugly, but that **gallon** the horse ain't too bad."*

gar·den (gärd´-in), *n. and adv.* the bringing forth of a militia armed for the purposes of maintaining or restoring order. *"That riot was so bad they had to call the National **garden**."*

Geor·gia (jòrj´-ə), *n. and adj.* a phrase connecting a person named George to a direct object. *"Dick Cheney shot him, but I'm sure they're gonna give old **Georgia** hard time about it."*

gey·ser (gīz´-ər), *n. and v.* a judgment or declaration concerning a group of males. *"Those **geyser** idiots."*

GEYSER

GRANDIOSE

gon·do·lier (gän-də-lir´), *v.* movement toward, with the purpose of gazing wantonly. *"Old Cooter's gondolier at the cheerleaders practicing."*

go·pher (gō´-fər), *v. and prep.* to move forth with a specific purpose. *"Man, I think I broke my leg in that damned rodent hole. You're gonna have to gopher help."*

gour·met (gȯr-mā´), *n. and v.* concerning the possible actions of anyone with the surname Gore. *"Holy cow, they're sayin' Al gourmet try and run for president again."*

gran·di·ose (grand-ē-ōs´), *n. and v.* a male's obligation for one thousand dollars. *"It must be more than a grandiose those guys."*

gra·vy (grāv´-ē), *n. and pron.* concerning a male's re-action to or connection with a burial site. *"Soon as he gets near a **gravy** starts shakin'."*

ham·per (ham´-pər), *n. and prep.* a cooked pig and its ratio to every member of a group. *"We gotta ration 'cause we only got one **hamper** man."*

hand·i·cap (han´-di-kap), *n.* a covering for the head that adds convenience in use. *"Work is way better now, thanks to my **handicap**!"*

har·mo·ny (här´-mə-nē), *v. and n.* to cause dam-age to the speaker's mid-leg joint. *"If I don't pay them back by Tuesday, they're gonna **harmony**."*

HANDICAP

HERBIVORE

hea·then (hē´-thən), *n. and adv.* referring to the subsequent action of a male. *"After he said he was an atheist, **heathen** proceeded to take the Lord's name in vain."*

Heim·lich (hīm´-lik), *n. and v.* a person's declared intention to draw his or her tongue against a thing. *"After Mama gets through mixing the icing, **Heimlich** the spoon!"*

her·bi·vore (hər´-bə-vòr), *n. and conj.* concerning a female prior to an event. *"Unfortunately, he asked **herbivore** the accident."*

hill·side (hil-sīd´), *n. and v.* the predicted alliance of a male person. *"Don't ask her husband to back you . . . **hillside** with her every time."*

His·pan·ic (his-pa´-nik), *adj. and n.* the hysterical reaction of a male. *"I'm worried about Dr. Hernandez, 'cause **Hispanic** attacks are gettin' more frequent."*

hol·lan·daise (häl´-ən-dāz), *adj. and n.* a period of time in which one transported goods. *"I had a real sweet eighteen-wheeler back in my **hollandaise**."*

hon·es·ty (än´-əs-tē), *prep. and n.* into a position of rest upon a peg used in the opening play on any hole in the game of golf. *"If you want to drive all the way to the green, put your ball **honesty**."*

hon·or stu·dent (än´-ər stü´-dənt), *prep. and n.* for a female to be positioned over, and supported by, a pupil. *"Yeah, I knew piano lessons after midnight was weird, but I didn't suspect nothin' till I caught her **honor student**."*

HISPANIC

HORNET

Hoo·sier (hü´-zhər), *n. and v.* phrase used to inquire into another's relationship with someone. *"**Hoosier** daddy?"*

hor·net (hȯrn´-ət), *n. and pron.* a condition involving a brass instrument. *"Every night he plays that **hornet** keeps me up."*

Ii

ice cream (īs´-krēm), *n. and v.* to cry out verbally in a loud, shrieking tone. *"Every time Junior wins a race, **ice cream** so loud the neighbors call the police."*

Ida·ho (īd´-ə-hō), *n. and v.* to have declared the possession of a tool used for breaking apart earth. *"**Idaho**, but Barry borrowed it, and I ain't seen it since."*

in·cense (in´-sents), *conj. and n.* penny currency, in addition to other moneys. *"Just tell me what it's gonna cost me in dollars incense."*

in·cite (in-sīt´), *prep. and n.* indicating position within a visual or achievable range. *"Always keep your goals incite."*

in·fa·my (in´-fə-mē), *adv. and n.* another person's intent to exact physical punishment. *"Ever since I went on that crime spree, the cops have had it infamy."*

in·stinct (in´-stinkt), *prep. and n.* concerning the level of olfactory offensiveness. *"I'll give it an 8 in sound, and a 10 instinct."*

NATIONAL BURP
CHAMPIONSHIPS

INSTINCT

IRAQ; IRAN

In·u·it (in´-yü-ət), *conj. and n.* a pronouncement that another is to be the targeted object, usually within the context of a game. *"We're playing tag, **Inuit**."*

in·ward (in´-wərd), *prep. and n.* concerning the record of a person's verbalizations. *"A scout is trustworthy **inward** and deed."*

Iraq; Iran (i-rak´; i-ran´), *n.; v.* the ampleness of one's bosom; to compete for. *"If I had **Iraq** like hers, I'd **Iran** for Miss Tennessee, too."*

is·land (ī´-lənd), *n. and v.* to declare one's projected arrival. *"The plane takes off at two and **island** at seven."*

is·land·er (ī-lənd-ər), *n. and v.* to temporarily give to a female. *"If islander any more money, I'll be broke."*

jack·et (ja´-kət), *v. and n.* to raise a specified object on a sturdy portable device, using leverage. *"You can't change the tires until you jacket up."*

jest·er (jest´-ər), *adv. and n.* exclusive indication of a person who is connected to the one being spoken to. *"I'm not letting all y'all in, jester friend in the glasses."*

jour·ney (jər´-nē), *n.* a specified person's mid-leg joint. *"You hurt journey in that fight?"*

JESTER

KILOWATT

Ju·ly (jŭ-lī´), *n. and v.* interrogative regarding another's veracity. *"Why **July** about it?"*

Ju·pi·ter (jü´-pə-tər), *n. and v.* imperative regarding another's action, with an implied threat or warning. *"**Jupiter** stop jumpin' on the bed."*

jus·tice (jəs´-təs), *adv.* comparatively equal. *"That lawyer's case is **justice** good as the other guy's."*

Kk

kilo·watt (kil´-ə-wät), *v. and n.* interrogative as to the specific identity of an intended prey animal, with the objective of ending its life. *"Tell me one more time: we're goin' out to **kilowatt**?"*

kil·ter (kilt´-ər), *v. and n.* to end the life of a female. *"Betty drank so much gin last night, it coulda **kilter**."*

klep·to·ma·ni·ac (klep-tə-mā´-nē-ak), *v. and n.* to have collided with a person suffering from severe mental illness. *"When I was drivin' down by the nuthouse the other day, I think mighta **kleptomaniac**."*

knock·er (näk´-ər), *v. and n.* to disparage a female. *"Don't **knocker** till you tried her."*

Ll

lac·quer thin·ner (lak´-ər thin´-ər), *v. and adv.* to prefer less corporeal mass on a female. *"I still think Kirstie Alley's cute, but I **lacquer thinner**."*

KLEPTOMANIAC

LETTUCE

lar·i·at (ler´-ē-ət), *n. and prep.* interrogative regarding the location of a person named Laurence. *"Where's **lariat**?"*

let·ter·head (let´-ər-hed), *v. and n.* a suggested action concerning a certain female's cranial region. *"No worries, man, she's in here drunk every night—just **letterhead** hit the bar."*

let·tuce (let´-əs), *v. and n.* to suggest allowance of a specified action by a group. *"Oh Lord, I swear I will never play chicken again if You just please **lettuce** survive this!"*

li·chen (lī´-kən), *n. and v.* the result of an untruth. *"I don't care how long you been married, one big **lichen** wreck it all."*

Li·ma (lē´-mə), *v. and adj.* to demand that another abandon something or someone possessed or claimed by one. *"**Lima** girl alone!"*

Mm

mag·is·trate (ma´-jə-strāt), *n. and v.* declaration concerning the heterosexual orientation of a woman named Madge. *"Tanya's gay, but **magistrate**."*

maid·en (mād´-in), *v. and prep.* indicating the place of manufacture or creation of something. *"Seems like everything these days is **maiden** China."*

Man·hat·tan (man-ha´-tən), *interj. and v.* advice for action. *"**Manhattan** you better get outta here? You just hit that dude's car."*

Tanya

Madge

MAGISTRATE

MANNEQUIN

man·ne·quin (man´-i-kən), *n. and v.* regarding the abilities of a male person. *"Ain't a **mannequin** take my bear in a fight."*

man·tle (man´-təl), *n. and prep.* a male, up to a certain point in time. *"It's amazing, but that chick used to be a **mantle** she got that operation."*

man·u·script (man´-yə-skript), *interj. and n.* regarding another's written document, usually intended for dramatic performance. *"**Manuscript** was real good! Once I started readin' it I couldn't put it down!"*

mar·ket (märk´-ət), *v. and n.* to note something in writing. *"I'm getting married on March first, so make sure to **market** on your calendar."*

mar·su·pi·al (mär-süp´-ē-əl), *adj. and n.* a phrase suggesting an expected result of a male's ingestion of any additional quantity of a liquid food made with cooked meats or vegetables. *"If he eats any **marsupial** explode."*

mas·cara (mas-ker´-ə), *v.* to assume affection for. *"I don't know if you realize it, Bill, but Jenny **mascara** lot for you."*

mass (mas´), *adj. and n.* one's own backside. *"I've got to go on a diet. **Mass** is the size of a barn."*

mat·a·dor (mat´-ə-dòr), *n., v., and n.* a phrase declaring one's proximity to a swinging or sliding barrier used to bar or allow passage into or out of a structure or between rooms. *"**Matador**, man, but it's locked."*

MARSUPIAL

MIDGET

mate (māt´), *n. and v.* a declaration that one has sur-passed seven but not yet reached nine years of exis-tence. *"When they asked me how old I was, I said mate."*

May·ber·ry (mā´-ber-ē), *v.* a possible option per-taining to the entombment of someone or something. *"They Mayberry her next to her mother."*

mel·a·no·ma (mel-ə-nō´-mə), *n. and v.* to profess knowledge of something, such as another's feelings or intentions, when speaking to a person named Melvin. *"Melanoma mole looks funny, but I'm going to the tan-ning parlor anyway."*

midg·et (mi´-jət), *adj. and n.* a term regarding one's relation who is inflicted with mental deficiencies. *"Midget brother just drowned my truck."*

min·is·try (min´-əs-trē), *n. and v.* a declaration that one is located in the upper parts of a woody perennial plant with an elongated single stem. *"Look up, Reverend, ministry!"*

mis·take (mis-tāk´), *n. and v.* to command an unmarried female person to seize or capture something. *"Please, mistake the picture!"*

mi·to·sis (mī-tōs´-əs), *n. and v.* the state of the digits of one's foot. *"After all that walkin', mitosis sore."*

moan (mōn´), *n. and v.* to declare one's intentions. *"I don't care how big her old man is, moan ask her out."*

MISTAKE

MONORAIL

mob·ster (mäb´-stər), *n. and v.* an unruly crowd causing a disruption. *"Once they started drinkin', I saw that **mobster** up a pack of trouble."*

mon·i·tor (män´-ət-ər), *n., v., and conj.* a declaration as to two alternatives for one's placement. *"They already picked the team, Steve . . . either **monitor** not."*

mono·rail (män´-ə-rāl), *n., v., and adv.* stating the authenticity or intensity of one's current state. *"No way am I folding now, baby, **monorail** streak."*

mo·to·cross (mōt´-ō-krȯs), *n. and prep.* a water-filled trench used around a structure to prevent access from one side to the other. *"If your home is a castle, you should put a **motocross** your whole yard."*

mus·tache (məs´-stash), *v.* to urge secretive storage. *"Our collective band of ne'er-do-wells **mustache** our ill-gotten gains in a suitable hiding spot to keep the authorities from discerning their whereabouts, what ho?"*

mu·ti·neer (myüt-ən-ir´), *n. and prep.* the presence, at a particular place, of a person who is unable to speak. *"You better fetch a pen and paper if you want any answers—there's a **mutineer**."*

Nn

nar·row (na´-rō), *conj. and n.* in addition to a shafted projectile with a pointed or sharpened end. *"Sure wish I hadn't bought Kenny that bow **narrow**."*

ne·gate (ni-gāt´), *n.* a swinging barricade. *"Open **negate** and let me in!"*

NARROW

NEVADA

neu·ter (nü´-tər), *adv. and prep.* unfamiliar with. *"I'm neuter town, so I get lost a lot."*

Ne·va·da (nə-va´-də), *adv. and v.* to not ever have possessed. *"Believe it or not, I Nevada girl to call my own."*

nin·com·poop (nin´-kəm-püp), *adv. and v.* to subsequently move toward and defecate. *"He barks all day, nincompoop on my lawn at night!"*

no·ble (nō´-bul), *adj. and n.* completely without prevarication. *"That tree jumped right out in front of me, Judge, noble."*

no·bler (nō´-blər), *adj. and n.* without any obscuring smear or indistinctness. *"Ain't had **nobler** in my vision since I got laser surgery."*

noc·turne (näkt´-ərn), *v. and n.* to have impregnated at least two females. *"I think I may have **nocturne** her sister up!"*

no·el (nō-el´), *adj. and n.* the absence of a pit that supplies water. *"Hell no, I didn't see **noel** until I fell into it."*

nosy (nō´-zē), *v. and n.* to cognitively understand something regarding a male. *"I don't mean to be a buttinsky here, but am I the only guy who **nosy** cain't swim?"*

NOCTURNE

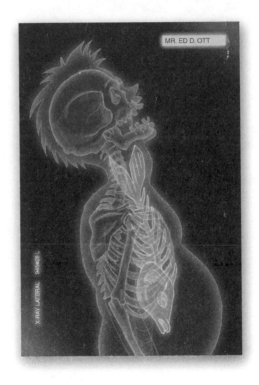

OFFICIATE

Oo

of·fense (ə-fens´), *n.* a barricade. *"No offense, ma'am, but I'm putting up offense."*

of·fi·ci·ate (ə-fish´-ē-āt), *n. and v.* an aquatic animal consumed by a male. *"I'm guessing Pete choked—musta been officiate."*

ol·fac·to·ry (äl-fak´-tə-rē), *adj. and n.* an aging manufacturing facility. *"They're closin' down the olfactory on account of it smells so bad."*

ol·ive (ä´-liv), *n. and v.* to proclaim one's existence, especially as under certain circumstances. *"I'll never drink another martini if olive to be a hundred."*

on·line (ȯn-līn´), *adv. and v.* to continue telling an untruth. *"I saw you lookin' at Internet porn, so don't go online to me about it."*

op·press (ə-pres´), *n. and v.* one's application of steady, bodily force. *"So you're tellin' me if oppress that button, this little old room we're in is gonna slide up the side of the building?!"*

Or·eos (ȯr´-ē-ōz), *n. and v.* a male person's obligations, under certain circumstances. *"Either he brings back my lawn mower, Oreos me two hundred dollars!"*

or·i·gin (ȯr´-ə-jən), *conj. and n.* involving a choice between any item and a colorless alcoholic beverage made from distilled grain spirits flavored with juniper berries. *"Hmmm . . . should I have a blueberry daiquiri origin fizz?"*

OPPRESS

OVERT

os·trich (ä´-strich), *n. and v.* one engaging in the act of muscular elongation. *"I'll be there soon as **ostrich** my legs."*

out·stand·ing (aut-stan´-ding), *adv. and v.* assuming an erect posture in a place away from the interior of an inhabitable structure. *"That moron's **outstanding** in the middle of the street."*

overt (ō-vərt´), *adv. and n.* above or across a thing. *"We tried to drive **overt**, but we got stuck."*

owl (au´-əl), *adv. and v.* interrogative addressing future means. *"**Owl** we get in if we ain't got keys?"*

Pa·cif·ic (pə-siʹ-fĭk), *adj.* exact; in precise detail. *"He asked if I'd ever shot anyone, and I asked him if he could be more **Pacific**."*

pad·dle (padʹ-əl), *n. and v.* the predicted state of a residence. *"I've looked at many places, but this **paddle** be perfect."*

par·a·dise (perʹ-ə-dīs), *n.* two matched, numbered cubes for use for gaming. *"He thinks he's special since he got that fuzzy **paradise** hanging from his rearview mirror."*

para·nor·mal (par-ə-nŏrʹ-məl), *n. and adj.* two things or persons representative of the mean or otherwise average. *"Don't pay any attention to them, Jane, I think you've got a **paranormal** kids."*

PARANORMAL

PASTEURIZE

pas·teur·ize (pas´-chər-īz), *prep. and n.* moving beyond or to the other side of the ocular organs of the person addressed by the speaker. *"I don't know how you missed that duck, Dick . . . it flew right **pasteurize**."*

pat·ter (pat´-ər), *v. and n.* to perform a quick, gentle touch, with the flat of the hand, upon a female. *"Sometimes, to let her know I'm available, when my wife walks by I just **patter** on the butt."*

phar·ma·cy (färm´-ə-sē), *n. and v.* the speaker's visual perception regarding a plot of land used for growing crops or raising livestock. *"Let's hunt behind Jerry's barn, cuz every time I'm at his **pharmacy** deer."*

play·wright (plā´-rīt), *v. and adv.* to engage in recreational activity properly. *"I swear I'm gonna bust your heads wide open if you boys don't quit fightin' and **playwright**."*

pok·er (pok´-ər), *v. and adj.* to jab a female. *"Don't swing that stick at your sister, boy . . . you might **poker** eye out."*

poo·dle (pü´-dil), *v. and prep.* to defecate up to a particular future time. *"Feed that dog Mexican food and he'll **poodle** next Tuesday."*

pop·u·late (päp´-yə-lāt), *n. and adv.* the tardiness of a direct male progenitor. *"**Populate**—I been waitin' for over an hour!"*

port (pȯrt´), *v. and n.* to cause the gravitational transfer of a previously mentioned liquid out of a container. *"Says here, 'Expires 10/02'—should I chuck it or **port**?"*

PORT

PRIOR

por·tion (pȯrsh´-ən), *n. and conj.* in addition to an automobile such as a Boxster or Carrera. *"What's the problem, Officer?" "Well, to start, your **portion** you was doin' a hundred and twenty in a school zone."*

po·ta·to (pət-tā´-tō), *conj. and n.* the inability of a group, regardless of other factors. *"They see us talkin', **potato** know what we're sayin'."*

pre·ced·ed (prē-sēd´-əd), *v.* previously sown. *"They ain't ours, Officer. When we bought the house, all those pot plants was **preceded**."*

pri·or (prī´-ər), *v. and n.* to forcibly move a female, using leverage. *"His first wife was so fat, you couldn't **prior** out of the front seat with a crowbar."*

pro·to·col (prō´-tə-kȯl), *n. and v.* a person, paid for his or her expertise, initiating communication. *"Maybe I'll get a **protocol** you and set up some lessons."*

Qq

quar·ter·back (kwȯr´-tər-bak), *n. and adv.* the return of coined currency worth twenty-five cents. *"I'll stop kickin' this thing when I get my **quarterback**."*

quea·sy (kwē´-zē), *v. and adv.* to request restrained enthusiasm. *"**Queasy** on them oysters, boy, you're makin' me sick."*

ques·tion·naire (kwes´-chən-er), *n. and adj.* a particular solicitation of information. *"Where'd I park my car? Now that's a real good **questionnaire**."*

PROTOCOL

RATTLE

Rr

rain·bows (rān´-bōz), *v. and adj.* watery precipitation and its relation to a thing or event connected to a person named Beauregard. *"I sure hope it don't **rainbows** weddin' out."*

rat·tle (rat´-il), *n. and v.* predicted behavior from a large rodent of the family Muridae. *"We need to clear the food off this table, or a **rattle** get at it."*

re·bate (rē´-bāt), *v.* to replace food intended to lure prey, as in a trap or on a hook. *"That fish took your worm, so you're gonna have to **rebate**."*

rig·or·ous (rig´-ər-əs), *n. and conj.* a choice between a vehicle and a group that includes the speaker. *"I know you hate to abandon the boat, but it's your **rigorous**!"*

Ro·lex (rōl´-leks), *v. and n.* to move a person who goes by a nickname for Alex by either turning him over and over or in a hand-propelled wheeled vehicle. *"Every night after the bar closes, we gotta **Rolex** home in a wheelbarrow."*

rose·wood (rōz´-wúd), *n. and v.* agreed-upon activity by a woman named after a flower. *"Tina wouldn't, but **rosewood**, so I married Rose."*

rub·ber (rəb´-ər), *v. and n.* to move one's hand firmly, in a repeated pattern, upon a female. *"To give a massage, **rubber** shoulders like this."*

run·ner (rən´-ər), *v. and n.* to repel a female. *"I tried treatin' my girlfriend bad, but I can't seem to **runner** off."*

ROLEX

SAHARA

rus·tle (rəs´-əl), *n. and v.* predicted actions of a person named Russell. *"Leave your wallet out like that and I guarantee old **rustle** steal it."*

Ss

Sa·ha·ra (sə-her´-ə), *v. and n.* a phrase concerning the state or condition of filaments growing from one's epidermis. *"The shave was fine, but it'**Sahara** got a problem with."*

saint (sānt´), *n. and v.* to deny or argue against the state of something. *"You just keep on driving along, dude, but I'm tellin' you, **saint** the right way!"*

salm·on (sam´-ən), *n. and conj.* connecting a person named Samuel to other persons or things. *"**Salmon** his fishin' buddies have got to leave right now!"*

sat·is·fied (sad´-əs-fīd), *adj. and n.* concerning one's feelings of sorrow. *"When Ralph split with Sadie, I was as **satisfied** divorced her myself."*

sat·u·rate (sat´-chər-rāt), *v. and n.* interrogative about whether or not payment for services rendered is standard. *"**Saturate**, or are you gonna charge me double once you get the job?"*

sa·vory (sāv´-ər-ē), *v. and conj.* concerning alternatives for a male person and his setting aside of currency for later use. *"He better learn to **savory** will be broke when he's old."*

sea·weed (sē´-wēd), *v. and n.* to encourage comprehension of the circumstances experienced by the speaker and others. *"We didn't mean to break into your place, but . . . **seaweed** been outside in the cold for a long time, and we was freezing."*

SEAWEED

SEDITION

se·di·tion (si-diʹ-shən), *adj. and n.* a specific calcu-
lation of the sum of two or more numbers. *"I don't
mean to complain, ma'am, but* **sedition** *is real hard!"*

se·di·tious (sed-diʹ-shəs), *v. and n.* to have verbal-
ized the common name for flat-bottomed or concave
containers used to serve food. *"He asked if I wanted to
make dinner or do the dishes, and I* **seditious***."*

se·ño·ra (sān-yȯrʹ-ə), *v. and n.* regarding current
pronouncements about the person being addressed.
"Everybody used to say you was an idiot, but now they
señora *dang fool."*

sen·ti·men·tal (sent-ə-menʹ-təl), *v. and adj.* to
have caused telepathic delivery. *"I could pick which
card you're thinkin' of, if you* **sentimental** *picture to me."*

sep·a·rate (sep´-ər-āt), *prep. and v.* with the exclu-
sion of a female's consumption. *"Me and her was supposed to share our Happy Meals, **separate** all the fries."*

se·rum (sir´-əm), *v. and n.* to char the exterior of
more than one thing. *"If you want the steaks to stay
juicy, you gotta **serum**."*

shel·lac (shəl-lak´), *n. and v.* a female's future affection for. *"Tell you what, **shellac** you a lot better if you
take a bath."*

shud·der (shəd´-ər), *v.* indicating regret for a thing
or action not done. *"I **shudder** ducked when that guy
yelled, 'Duck!' "*

SEPARATE

SIOUX FALLS

shunt (shənt´), *v. and adv.* indicating that a thing or action was the incorrect one. *"My husband's home—I told you you **shunt** have come over!"*

side·burns (sīd´-bərnz), *n. and v.* a surface that is afire. *"Leave it on the grill until that **sideburns**."*

Sioux Falls (sü´-fȯlz), *n. and v.* a person named Susan going from a high position to a lower one because of gravitational pull. *"Sue drinks, **Sioux Falls**."*

si·nus (sīn´-əs), *v. and n.* to make a mark of identity needed as proof of approval, for a group. *"Money for medical experiments? Heck yeah, **sinus** up!"*

snot (snät´), *n. and v.* negating the state of being of a thing. *"Officer, I'm really sorry. I could have sworn that was the guy who cut me off in traffic, but maybe snot."*

so·lar (sōl´-ər), *v. and adj.* to effect a change of ownership, in exchange for currency, of a thing possessed by a female. *"I hear old lady Johnson finally solar house."*

sold (sōld´), *adv. and adj.* emphasizing the length of existence. *"If I were a little drunker and she weren't sold, I'd most definitely take a crack at her."*

spa (spä´), *v. and n.* interrogative regarding one's direct male progenitor. *"I know Ma's around, but spa here?"*

SOLD

STARSTRUCK

spear (spir´), *n. and v.* stating the presence of an alcoholic beverage made by using yeast to ferment malt and hops. *"We ain't got no wine here, honey. **Spear** or nothin'."*

spec·ta·tors (spek´-tā-tərz), *v. and n.* to presuppose an encounter with potatoes. *"What will they serve with the roast? I **spectators** and beans."*

star·struck (stär´-strək), *adj., n., and v.* coming into violent contact with a male person's circular rubber wheel covering. *"He got the blowout when **starstruck** that speed bump."*

strive (strīv´), *n. and v.* a phrase suggesting that one and others operate a motor vehicle; usually used during inebriation. *"Well, we done finished off the keg, so **strive** to Alaska!"*

stu·pid (stüp´-əd), *n. and v.* to get into a lower position because of the state of a thing. *"I told him, 'Kyle, you better **stupid** is really low.'"*

sui·cide (sü´-ə-sīd), *n. and v.* to agree with the opinion of or position taken by a person named Susan. *"I've heard his side of the story, but it's **suicide** with."*

sun·set (sən´-set), *n. and v.* a male offspring having made a statement. *"I never saw it, but my **sunset** it was the biggest fish he'd ever laid his eyes on."*

su·per (süp´-ər), *n. and conj.* used to indicate a choice between a liquid food made with cooked meats and/or vegetables and another thing. *"**Super** salad?"*

STUPID

SYNTHESIZE

sweat·er (swet´-ər), *v. and adj.* to be intimidated by something of a female's. *"Don't **sweater** rude comments. Just go ahead and ask her out."*

syn·the·size (sin´-thə-sīz), *n. and v.* a condition pertaining to a thing's mass or quantity. *"It ain't the size of the dog in the fight, **synthesize** of the fight in the dog."*

tab·leau (tab-lō´), *n. and adj.* a phrase pertaining to controlling the extent of a bill of sale. *"I ain't buyin' another round, 'cause I'm tryin' to keep my **tableau**."*

tal·on (ta´-lən), *v.* to be revealing information verbally. *"I'm **talon** you, it was an eagle, not a hawk."*

tee·pee (tē´-pē), *n.* urination caused by drinking the brewed leaves of *Camellia sinensis*. *"I love drinkin' tea, but after about half a cup I gotta take a **teepee**."*

tele·mar·ket·ing (tel´-ə-mär-kə-ting), *v. and adj.* to make a statement to someone or something involved in advertising. *"I once had to **telemarketing** guy that if he called my house one more time I'd hunt him down and shoot his phone."*

tele·path (tel´-ə-path), *conj. and n.* up to a certain time, with regard to a route. *"I ain't hiking no more **telepath** is chosen."*

Tel·es·tra·tor (tel´-əs-strāt-ər), *v. and n.* with an implied threat, to command a person to verbalize without prevarication. *"Enough of the bull, boy. Tell us the story and **Telestrator** else."*

TELEMARKETING

TENSION

tele·vise (tel´-əv-īz), *v. and conj.* to determine one's current state. *"I'm so drunk I can't even **televise** happy or sad."*

ten·e·ment (ten´-ə-mənt), *n. and v.* to intend an integer over nine and under eleven. *"Did I say five? It was **tenement**."*

ten·sion (ten´-shən), *n.* mental focus. *"My wife's mad at me 'cause I don't pay her no **tension**."*

ter·race (te´-rəs), *v. and pron.* to pull apart some-thing belong to a male. *"As soon as she saw him she tried to **terrace** clothes off."*

ter·rain (tə-rān´), *v.* to precipitate. *"They're sayin' it's supposed **terrain** this weekend."*

ter·ri·fy (tər´-əf-ī), *v. and conj.* to rip apart as a result of certain actions one might take. *"My skirt's so tight, I'm scared it'll **terrify** bend over."*

tes·ti·fy (test´-əf-ī), *n. and conj.* a written examination, in relation to certain actions one might take. *"I would have studied harder for that **testify** had known it was for half our grade."*

Tif·fa·ny (tif´-ən-ē), *n. and conj.* a fight, with an ensuing reaction by a male. *"My dad and me had a **Tiffany** done cut me out of his will."*

time (tīm´), *v. and n.* to fasten things together with a knot. *"Don't know what the hell's wrong with my shoes, but I can't seem to **time**."*

TIME

TORTURE

tor·ture (tor´-chər), *n. and v.* phrase concerning a person's flame used for lighting a dark area. *"I think there's something wrong with that **torture** holding."*

tram·po·line (tramp´-pəl-lēn), *n. and v.* a prediction that a destitute person or sexually promiscuous woman will rest against a thing or person. *"First that **trampoline** on ya—then she'll steal your wallet."*

trem·or (trem´-ər), *v. and adj.* to cut or shorten something belonging to a female. *"I got all shook up when Cassie asked me to **tremor** back hair."*

trip (trip´), *v.* to forcibly tear apart. *"First time I saw my wife I wanted **trip** her dress off and get busy."*

tsu·na·mi (sù-nä´-mē), *conj. and adv.* indicating the reason for an action one is about to take. *"My dang TV just broke, **tsunami** gotta go get a new one."*

tu·na (tün´-ə), *v. and adj.* to adjust for proper functioning. *"That boy don't say much, but he sure can **tuna** TV right."*

Uu

ud·der (ə´-dər), *adj.* referring to any person or thing that is not the one specified. *"My kid won't drink any milk **udder** than chocolate."*

uni·son (yü´-nə-sən), *n. and conj.* the person being addressed, plus their male offspring. *"Everyone said you was shootin' blanks, man—I never expected to see **unison**."*

TUNA

UTILIZE

unit·ed (yu̇-nī′-təd), *n. and v.* a British subject being asked about his status regarding a nonhereditary title for excellent public service and merit. *"Hey,* ***united*** *yet?"*

up·raise (əp-rāz′), *prep. and adj.* a vulgar insult to a person named Raymond referring to placing a thing where the sun doesn't shine. *"Up yours, Pete . . . and while I'm at it,* ***upraise****, too!"*

urol·o·gist (yu̇r-äl′-ə-jist), *n. and v.* a phrase claiming that a group is merely some lesser thing; usually used for the purpose of insult. *"****Urologist**** a bunch of sissies!"*

uti·lize (yü′-təl-īz), *n. and conj.* a connecting phrase concerning the speaker, a temporal condition, and the person being spoken to. *"I was scared to talk to* ***utilize*** *all grown up."*

Vv

va·cant (vā´-kənt), *n. and v.* a group's inability to do something. *"If **vacant** pay, **vacant** stay."*

ven·ture cap·i·tal (ven´-chər-ka´-pə-til), *adj. and n.* the principal or central place for exciting, extraordinary, and unexpected things. *"I'm tellin' you, man, Las Vegas is the **venture capital** of the whole world!"*

Ve·nus (vē´-nəs), *conj. and n.* indicating action conditional on that of a male plus other persons or things connected to him. *"I'll only go **Venus** friends go."*

vest·ed in·ter·est (vest´-əd-in´-trəst), *n. and v.* a short, sleeveless upper-body garment and the possible curiosity or attention it inspires. *"That **vested interest** me more if Pamela Anderson was wearing it."*

VESTED INTEREST

VETERAN

vet·er·an (vet´-ə-rən), *n. and v.* concerning a re-
tired soldier or a doctor who administers medical care
to animals and the fast pace of his movement. *"That's
the same **veteran** over my foot with his Rascal!"*

Ww

waf·fle (wäf´-əl), *n. and v.* future actions by or state
of a female spouse. *"If you want breakfast, my **waffle**
make it for you."*

walk·er (wòk´-ər), *v. and n.* to move on foot alongside a female. *"You be nice to Mamaw and **walker** to the
bus stop."*

wal·la·by (wäl´-lə-bē), *n. and v.* the predicted state
of the vertical part of a structure. *"That water's already
up to your waist, boy. Ain't no way that **wallaby** tall
enough to stop it."*

Weed Eat·er (wēd´-ē´-tər), *n. and v.* a phrase indicating past group mastication. *"Every time we were at your grannie's, **Weed Eater** cookies when she wasn't looking."*

wid·ow (wid´-ō), *n. and v.* a phrase promising future obligation for more than one person, including the speaker. *"I tell you, if you did us this favor, **widow** you big-time."*

Wif·fle (wif´-əl), *n. and v.* regarding the effects of experiencing an unpleasant odor. *"Ole Johnny stinks. One **Wiffle** knock you out."*

wig·gle (wig´-əl), *n. and v.* the future prospects for a prosthetic hairpiece. *"Think this **wiggle** fool 'em?"*

WIGGLE

WISDOM

Win·ches·ter (win´-ches-tər), *adv. and n.* at the time of events involving a person named Chester. *"We'll eat **Winchester** gets here."*

win·ter (wint´-ər), *v. and adj.* regarding the past movements of a female. *"She **winter** way and I went mine."*

wis·dom (wiz´-dəm), *v. and n.* to urinate more than one thing. *"My uncle had two kidney stones, but he **wisdom** both out."*

won·der (wən´-dər), *n. and prep.* indicating action concerning a specific person. *"If you need a good taxidermist, he's the **wonder** call."*

wrin·kle (rink´-əl), *n. and v.* a prediction involving an icy surface used for skating. *"I'm gonna throw my little girl an ice-skating party, and this **wrinkle** work great!"*

Xe·rox (zē´-räks), *v. and n.* to visually perceive solid mineral material. *"I ain't divin', 'cause I **Xerox**!"*

X-ray (eks´-rā), *n.* the former spouse of a person named Raymond. *"That's one of Ray's exes, but she ain't the **X-ray** was talkin' about."*

Yaht·zee (yät´-zē), *n. and v.* suggesting that a person visually perceive something. *"Oh man, **Yahtzee** the booty on Tiny's wife!"*

YAHTZEE

ZION

yar·mul·ke (yä´-mə-kə), *pron. and v.* a reference to something a person or group has created. *"No doubt about it, Rabbi Steinberg, **yarmulke** mean margarita."*

yel·low (ye´-lō), *interj.* a greeting. *"**Yellow!**"*

yon·der (yänd´-ər), *v. and n.* an involuntary intake of air and widening of the mouth, performed by a female. *"At her start of her interview she had the job, but then she **yonder** way out of it."*

Zi·on (zī´-ən), *n. and prep.* regarding the orientation of a male's ocular organ. *"He's had his **Zion** Betty-Lynn all night."*

ABOUT THE AUTHOR

JEFF FOXWORTHY is the largest-selling comedy-recording artist in history, a multiple Grammy Award nominee, and the bestselling author of more than twenty books. He is the star and executive producer of a new show on CMT, *Foxworthy's Big Night Out*. Prior to that he starred in and executive-produced the television series *Blue Collar TV*, which he also created. That television show came about due to the success of *Blue Collar Comedy Tour: The Movie*, which has sold more than 4 million units. The sequel, *Blue Collar Comedy Tour Rides Again*, has exceeded 3.6 million units in sales. The Blue Collar boys reunited to shoot *Blue Collar Comedy Tour: One for the Road* at the Warner Theatre in Washington, D.C., their final appearance together. Jeff also has an HBO special and two Showtime specials to his credit. His syndicated weekly radio show, *The Foxworthy Countdown*, is carried in more than 220 markets across the United States.

Offstage and -screen, Jeff has helped the Duke University Children's Hospital raise millions of dollars over the past ten years and is the honorary chairman of the Duke Children's Classic Golf Tournament. A Georgia native, he lives with his wife and two daughters in Atlanta.